Skills Practice

KS2 Success

10-MINUTE TESTS

Maths

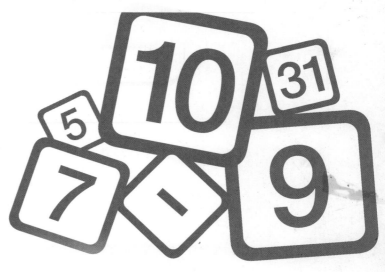

Paul Broadbent

Sample page

clear instructional text   topic being covered   test number for quick reference

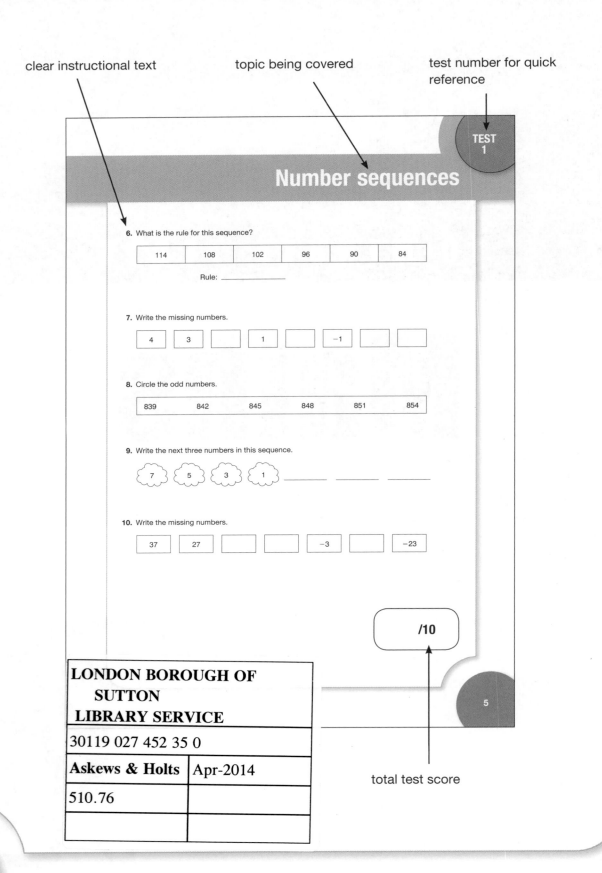

TEST 1

Number sequences

6. What is the rule for this sequence?

| 114 | 108 | 102 | 96 | 90 | 84 |

Rule: _____

7. Write the missing numbers.

| 4 | 3 | | 1 | | −1 | | |

8. Circle the odd numbers.

| 839 | 842 | 845 | 848 | 851 | 854 |

9. Write the next three numbers in this sequence.

7 5 3 1 _____ _____ _____

10. Write the missing numbers.

| 37 | 27 | | | −3 | | −23 |

/10

5

total test score

Contents

Number sequences

1. Write the next three numbers in this sequence.

14	19	24	29	34			

2. Write the missing numbers.

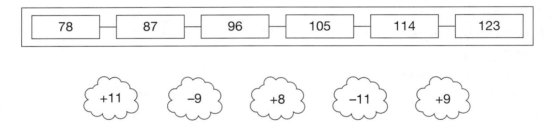

109   107   ⬡   ⬡   101   ⬡   ⬡

3. Circle the rule for this sequence.

78	87	96	105	114	123

+11   −9   +8   −11   +9

4. Colour the even numbers.

787	788	789	790	791	792	793

5. Write the missing numbers.

367 _____ 359 _____ _____ 347   343 _____

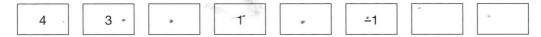

Number sequences

6. What is the rule for this sequence?

| 114 | 108 | 102 | 96 | 90 | 84 |

Rule: _____

7. Write the missing numbers.

| 4 | 3 | | 1 | | −1 | | |

8. Circle the odd numbers.

| 839 | 842 | 845 | 848 | 851 | 854 |

9. Write the next three numbers in this sequence.

7   5   3   1   _____ _____ _____

10. Write the missing numbers.

| 37 | 27 | | | −3 | | −23 |

/10

Place value

1. Write the missing numbers.

 a) 8145 = 8000 + 100 + _____ + _____

 b) 6239 = _____ + _____ + _____ + 9

2. What is the value of the digit 3 in the number 7384? Circle your answer.

  3000   300   3   30

3. Write these numbers using digits.

 a) six thousand two hundred and eighteen ➔ _____

 b) seven thousand and ninety-four   ➔ _____

4. What is 385 multiplied by 10? _____

5. Write the number shown on this abacus.

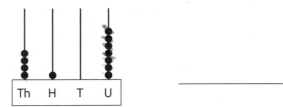

  _____

6. Write these numbers as words.

 a) 6008 ➔ _____

 b) 3970 ➔ _____

7. Draw the beads on this abacus to show the number 3058.

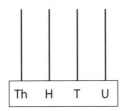

| Th | H | T | U |

8. Write the numbers coming out of this machine.

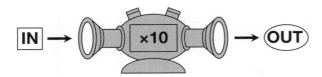

IN	328	900	405	780	649
OUT					

9. Write the numbers coming out of this machine.

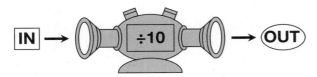

IN	2400	3000	7510	2660	4090
OUT					

10. Write these in thousands, hundreds, tens and ones.

a) 7412 = _____ + _____ + _____ + _____

b) 5946 = _____ + _____ + _____ + _____

/10

Ordering numbers

1. Circle the largest number in each pair.

a)
3085
3100

b)
2101
2011

c)
5990
5967

2. Write the sign < or > for each pair of numbers.

a) 4717 [   ] 4910

b) 5111 [   ] 5109

3. Tick the smallest amount in this set.

6785 g ☐   6077 g ☐   7099 g ☐   6699 g ☐   6799 g ☐

4. Write these numbers in order, starting with the smallest.

4929   4299   5102

5015   5000

_____

5. Write the half-way number on this number line.

| 2010 | | | 2110 |

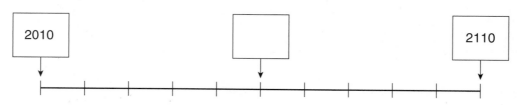

Ordering numbers

6. These numbers should be in order. Colour the two numbers that have been swapped.

2799	2802	2801	2800	2803	2804

7. I am thinking of a whole number. It is greater than 3099 and less than 3101.

   What number am I thinking of? _____

8. Write these lengths in order, starting with the smallest.

 3056 m   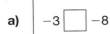 4100 m   3988 m    4078 m   3065 m

   _____

9. Write the sign < or > for each pair of numbers.

   a) −3 ☐ −8   b) −4 ☐ −1

10. Write these temperatures in order, starting with the lowest.

 −8°C   4°C   −3°C

   2°C   0°C   −1°C

   _____

   /10

Rounding numbers

1. Round these numbers to the nearest 100.

   a) 3840 → _____

   b) 7259 → _____

2. Draw lines to join these numbers to the nearest 10.

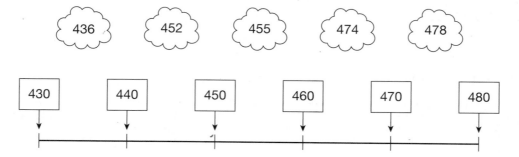

   | 436 | | 452 | | 455 | | 474 | | 478 |

   | 430 | | 440 | | 450 | | 460 | | 470 | | 480 |

3. Round these amounts to the nearest pound.

   a) £3.48 → _____

   b) £5.09 → _____

   c) £8.57 → _____

4. Write two numbers that would round to 6200 to the nearest 100.

   _____   _____

5. Round the number the arrow is pointing to, to the nearest 100 g.

   [_____] g

   1000 g   1500 g   2000 g

Rounding numbers

6. Round these numbers to the nearest 10.

    a) 7465 → _____

    b) 3092 → _____

7. Round each number to the nearest 10 to give an approximate answer.

    a) 138 + 263 → _____

    b) 452 + 336 → _____

8. Draw lines to join these numbers to the nearest 100.

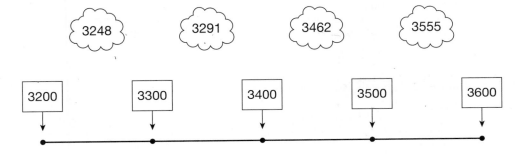

9. Round these to the nearest 10 metres.

    a) 7484 m → _____

    b) 3066 m → _____

10. Round each number to the nearest 10 then calculate to give an approximate answer.

    a) 458 − 139 → _____

    b) 773 − 347 → _____

/10

Decimals

1. Write these as decimals.

   a) $\frac{7}{10}$ → ▢   b) $\frac{3}{10}$ → ▢   c) $\frac{8}{10}$ → ▢

2. Write the decimals on this number line.

   0   1

3. Change these decimals to tenths.

   a) 0.1 → ▢   b) 0.6 → ▢   c) 0.9 → ▢

4. Draw lines to match these decimals to the fractions.

   | 8.3 | 9.7 | 8.1 | 9.4 | 8.9 |

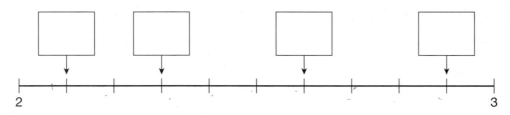

   $8\frac{1}{10}$ $9\frac{4}{10}$ $9\frac{7}{10}$ $8\frac{9}{10}$ $8\frac{3}{10}$

5. Write the decimals on this number line.

   2   3

Decimals

6. Draw lines to match these decimals to the fractions.

| 0.35 | 0.04 | 0.55 | 0.44 | 0.53 |

$\frac{44}{100}$ $\frac{4}{100}$ $\frac{53}{100}$ $\frac{35}{100}$ $\frac{55}{100}$

7. Write these as decimals.

a) $\frac{37}{100}$ → _____   b) $\frac{85}{100}$ → _____   c) $\frac{9}{100}$ → _____

8. Write these in order, starting with the lowest value.

| £6.45 | £6.80 | £6.54 | £6.08 | £6.58 |

_____

9. Write the decimals on this number line.

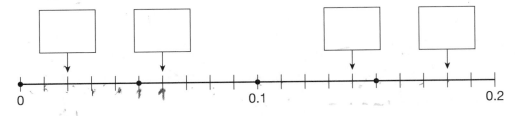

10. Write the answer as a decimal number.

$50 + 7 + \frac{3}{10} + \frac{9}{100} =$ _____

/10

Fractions

1. Write the fraction shaded for each of these shapes.

a)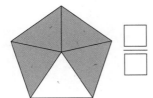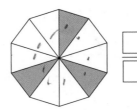

b)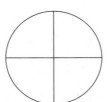

c)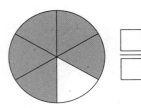

2. Colour $\frac{3}{4}$ of each of these shapes.

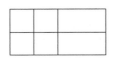

3. Tick the shape that is divided into sixths.

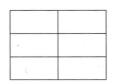

4. Shade this circle to show $\frac{2}{3}$.

5. Which fraction is larger, $\frac{2}{5}$ or $\frac{4}{5}$?

_____

Fractions

6. Write the fraction shaded for each of these shapes.

a)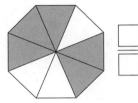

b)

c)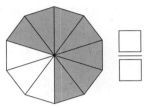

7. Write the fraction that must be added to each of these fractions to make one whole.

a) $\dfrac{3}{5} + \dfrac{\square}{\square} = 1$

b) $\dfrac{5}{6} + \dfrac{\square}{\square} = 1$

8. Colour the shapes to show the fractions.

a) $\dfrac{5}{6}$

b) $\dfrac{2}{5}$

9. Use > or < to complete these.

a)

$\dfrac{3}{7} \; \square \; \dfrac{5}{7}$

b)

$\dfrac{1}{3} \; \square \; \dfrac{1}{5}$

10. Write these fractions on the number line.

$4\dfrac{1}{4}$ $3\dfrac{1}{2}$ $4\dfrac{3}{4}$ $3\dfrac{1}{4}$ $3\dfrac{3}{4}$

3   5

/10

Equivalent fractions

Write each fraction shaded in two ways.

1. a) 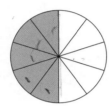 $\dfrac{1}{\boxed{}} = \dfrac{\boxed{}}{6}$

b) 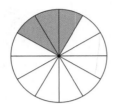 $\dfrac{1}{\boxed{}} = \dfrac{\boxed{}}{12}$

2. a) 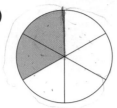 $\dfrac{1}{\boxed{}} = \dfrac{\boxed{}}{10}$

b) 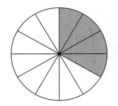 $\dfrac{1}{\boxed{}} = \dfrac{\boxed{}}{12}$

3. a) 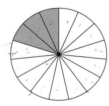 $\dfrac{1}{\boxed{}} = \dfrac{\boxed{}}{15}$

b) 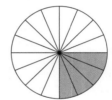 $\dfrac{1}{\boxed{}} = \dfrac{\boxed{}}{16}$

Cross out the fraction that is not equivalent to the others in the set.

4.

 $\dfrac{5}{10}$ $\dfrac{3}{6}$ $\dfrac{6}{15}$

$\dfrac{4}{8}$ $\dfrac{9}{18}$

5.

$\dfrac{3}{9}$ $\dfrac{10}{30}$ $\dfrac{4}{10}$

$\dfrac{2}{6}$ $\dfrac{6}{18}$

Equivalent fractions

6. Colour each shape to make the shading equivalent to $\frac{3}{4}$. Write the fractions shown.

a)

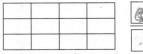

b)

7. Complete this equivalent fraction chain.

$$\frac{1}{3} = \frac{2}{\boxed{}} = \frac{\boxed{}}{9} = \frac{4}{\boxed{}} = \frac{\boxed{}}{15}$$

Complete these.

8. $\dfrac{3}{\boxed{}} = \dfrac{\boxed{}}{8}$

9. $\dfrac{\boxed{}}{3} = \dfrac{4}{\boxed{}}$

10. $\dfrac{4}{\boxed{}} = \dfrac{\boxed{}}{10}$

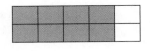

/10

Ratio and proportion

These boxes of beads are in two colours: red and blue. The proportion of beads that are blue is always two in every five, or $\frac{2}{5}$. How many red and blue beads are there in each box?

1.

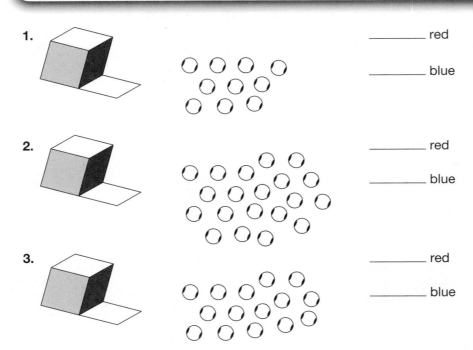

_____ red

_____ blue

2.

_____ red

_____ blue

3.

_____ red

_____ blue

4. Colour this grid so that there are two green squares to every one yellow square.

5. Colour this grid so that there are four green squares to every one yellow square.

Ratio and proportion

The tiles in a bathroom are black and white. Shade these tiles to make patterns to show the different ratios.

6. One black tile to every two white tiles

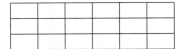

7. Two black tiles to every three white tiles

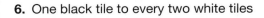

8. Three black tiles to every one white tile

9. In a bag of 15 apples, two out of every three of the apples are green.

How many of the apples are green? _____

10. In a box of 20 chocolates, three out of every five of the chocolates are toffees.

How many toffees are there altogether? _____

/10

Addition and subtraction facts

1. Write the missing numbers.

   a) 70 + ☐ = 130

   b) ☐ + 80 = 170

2. What is the difference between each pair of numbers?

   a)  160 90 → ☐

   b) 60 140 → ☐

3. Write the missing numbers. Each pair must total 1000.

   a) 500 + ☐

   b) 800 + ☐

   c) 300 + ☐

   d) 600 + ☐

4. Answer these.

   a) 18 − 9 = ☐

   b) 8 + 7 = ☐

   c) 17 − 8 = ☐

   d) 9 + 6 = ☐

5. Complete this addition grid.

+	90		80
	160		
40	130		
50		110	

Addition and subtraction facts

6. What is the total of 30, 90 and 40?

_____

7. Write the missing numbers.

a) [ ] − 50 = 70   **b)** 130 − [ ] = 70   **c)** [ ] − 90 = 50

8. Complete this number trail from 1000.

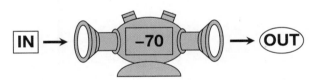

1000 —200→ ( ) —500→ ( ) —200→ ( ) —85→ ( )

9. This is a **−70** machine. Write the missing numbers in the table below.

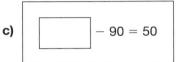

IN → −70 → OUT

IN	150		190		120
OUT		40		60	

10. I am thinking of a number. If I add 40 to it, the answer is 110.

What number am I thinking of? _____

/10

Multiplication and division facts

1. Write the missing numbers.

    a)   9 × _____ = 27   **b)**   _____ × 6 = 48   **c)**   4 × _____ = 28

2. Write four facts for this trio.

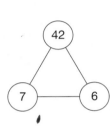

		×	6	=	
		×	7	=	
		÷	6	=	
		÷	7	=	

3. Answer these.

    a)   4 × 9 = _____   **b)**   8 × 5 = _____   **c)**   7 × 7 = _____

4. Answer these.

    a)   21 ÷ 3 = _____   **b)**   56 ÷ 8 = _____   **c)**   54 ÷ 6 = _____

5. Complete this multiplication grid.

×	4		8
9		45	
7			
	12		

Multiplication and division facts

6. Write four different facts for each number.

a)

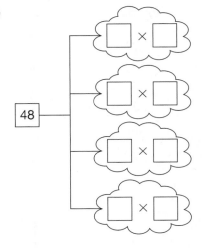

b)

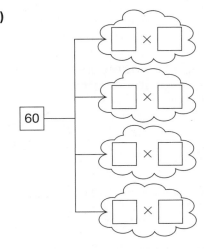

7. Which number between 30 and 40 can be divided exactly by 2, 3, 4, 6 and 9?

_____

8. I am thinking of a number. If I multiply it by 8, the answer is 56.

What number am I thinking of?_____

9. I am thinking of a number. If I divide it by 9, the answer is 5.

What number am I thinking of?_____

10. Draw lines to join each division to its matching remainder.

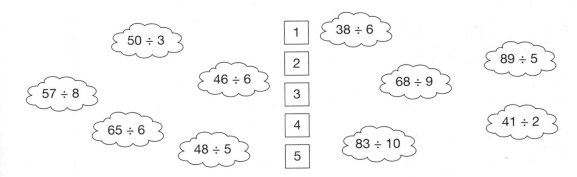

/10

Addition

1. Answer these.

   a) 38 + 41 = _____   b) 65 + 52 = _____   c) 83 + 72 = _____

Look at these five numbers.

 38   46   58   63   45

2. Which two numbers total 104? _____ and _____

3. Which two numbers total 101? _____ and _____

4. Write the missing numbers.

   a) 87 + _____ = 115   b) _____ + 74 = 123

5. Draw lines to join pairs of numbers that total 200.

   | 72 | | 135 | | 65 |

   | 138 | | 95 | | 62 |

   | 105 | | 128 |

Addition

6. Mrs Jones travels 68 km to a meeting. She then travels 39 km to her office and, finally, a further 43 km back home.

   How far does Mrs Jones travel in total?

   _____ km

7. Answer these.

   a) $\begin{array}{r} 2\ 8\ 4 \\ +\ 1\ 6\ 3 \\ \hline \\ \hline \end{array}$ **b)** $\begin{array}{r} 3\ 0\ 9 \\ +\ 2\ 5\ 7 \\ \hline \\ \hline \end{array}$ **c)** $\begin{array}{r} 5\ 4\ 7 \\ +\ 1\ 8\ 4 \\ \hline \\ \hline \end{array}$

8. Add each row and column to find the total in the bottom right-hand corner.

   a)

62	53	
29	47	

   b)

49	58	
71	93	

9. Write the missing digits.

   a) $\begin{array}{r} 3\ \square\ 5 \\ +\ 2\ 8\ \square \\ \hline \square\ 5\ 4 \end{array}$ **b)** $\begin{array}{r} \square\ 4\ 9 \\ +\ 3\ \square\ 6 \\ \hline 8\ 2\ \square \end{array}$

10. Matthew buys a tennis racket costing £34.80 and a tube of tennis balls costing £8.25. How much does he spend altogether?

    £_____

/10

Subtraction

1. Answer these.

    a) 97 − 38 = _____   **b)** 83 − 47 = _____

2. What is the difference between these three numbers? Write the answers in the boxes.

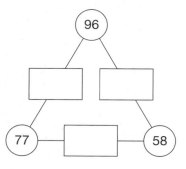

3. Write the missing digits.

    a)

$$
\begin{array}{r}
\boxed{}\,4\;3 \\
-\quad 8\;\boxed{} \\
\hline
1\;\boxed{}\;1 \\
\hline
\end{array}
$$

    b)

$$
\begin{array}{r}
3\;\boxed{}\;2 \\
-\quad 5\;\boxed{} \\
\hline
\boxed{}\;3\;5 \\
\hline
\end{array}
$$

4. The difference between two numbers is 92. If the largest number is 185, what is the other number?

_____

5. Draw lines to join pairs with a difference of 55.

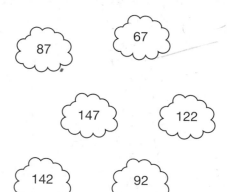

Subtraction

6. Write the missing numbers.

a) 82 – _____ = 24

b) _____ – 49 = 27

c) _____ – 38 = 39

d) 95 – _____ = 26

7. Write the difference between these numbers.

a)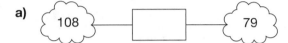

b)

8. I am thinking of a number. If I subtract 88 from it, the answer is 70.

What number am I thinking of? _____

9. Complete this subtraction chain.

10. Answer these.

a)
```
  3 4 9
– 1 7 4
───────
```

b)
```
  5 0 7
– 2 8 8
───────
```

c)
```
  4 2 3
– 1 6 9
───────
```

/10

Multiplication

1. This is a ×100 machine. Complete the table below.

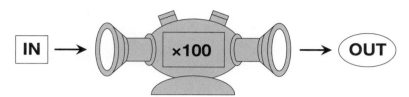

IN	14		22		40
OUT		3000		1700	

2. I am thinking of a number. When I multiply it by 11, the answer is 121.

   What number am I thinking of? _____

3. Answer these.

   a) 29 × 5 = ☐

   b) 34 × 6 = ☐

4. There are 24 hours in a day. How many hours are there in a week?

   _____ hours

5. Double each of these numbers.

   a)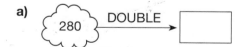

   b)

Multiplication

6. Answer these. ✓

a)

57 × 6

×	50	7
6		

→ [ ]

b)✓

84 × 9

×	80	4
9		

→ [ ]

7. A train ticket costs £57. What is the total cost of four tickets?

£ _____

8. Answer these.

a)   7 2
    ×   5
    _____

b)   6 8
    ×   7
    _____

c)   8 3
    ×   4
    _____

9. What number is double 660?

_____

10. In a chocolate factory, Choco-bars are put in packs of six. Each pack is put in a large box that holds 45 packs.

How many Choco-bars are there in each box?

_____

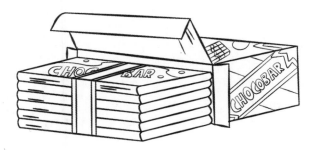

/10

Division

1. Answer these.

a) 27 ÷ 3 = _____

b) 46 ÷ 2 = _____

c) 42 ÷ 6 = _____

d) 65 ÷ 5 = _____

2. Halve each number and write the answer.

a) 108 → ☐

b) 146 → ☐

c) 134 → ☐

3. This is a ÷**10** machine. Complete the table below.

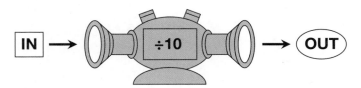

IN	370	900	740	810	620
OUT					

4. Answer these.

a) 4 ⟌ 48

b) 5 ⟌ 90

c) 6 ⟌ 84

5. Write the missing numbers in each of these.

a) ☐ ÷ 7 = 5

b) ☐ ÷ 8 = 7

c) 81 ÷ ☐ = 9

d) 54 ÷ ☐ = 6

Answer booklet: Maths 10-Minute Tests, age 8–9

Test 1
1. 39   44   49
2. 105   103   99   97
3. +9
4. 788   790   792
5. 363   355   351   339
6. −6
7. 2   0   −2   −3
8. 839   845   851
9. −1   −3   −5
10. 17   7   −13

Test 2
1. **a)** $8000 + 100 + \mathbf{40} + \mathbf{5}$
   b) $\mathbf{6000} + \mathbf{200} + \mathbf{30} + 9$
2. 300
3. **a)** 6218   **b)** 7094
4. 3850
5. 4107
6. **a)** six thousand and eight
   b) three thousand nine hundred and seventy
7.
8.

IN	328	900	405	780	649
OUT	**3280**	**9000**	**4050**	**7800**	**6490**

9.

IN	2400	3000	7510	2660	4090
OUT	**240**	**300**	**751**	**266**	**409**

10. **a)** $7000 + 400 + 10 + 2$
    b) $5000 + 900 + 40 + 6$

Test 3
1. **a)** 3100
   b) 2101
   c) 5990
2. **a)** $4717 < 4910$ **b)** $5111 > 5109$
3. 6077 g
4. 4299   4929   5000
   5015   5102
5. 2060
6. 2802   2800
7. 3100
8. 3056 m   3065 m
   3988 m   4078 m   4100 m
9. **a)** $-3 > -8$ **b)** $-4 < -1$
10. −8°C   −3°C   −1°C
    0°C   2°C   4°C

Test 4
1. **a)** 3800   **b)** 7300
2. 436 —— 440
   452 —— 450
   455 —— 460
   474 —— 470
   478 —— 480

3. **a)** £3   **b)** £5   **c)** £9
4. Check answers are between 6150 and 6249.
5. 1800 g
6. **a)** 7470   **b)** 3090
7. **a)** 400
   b) 790
8. 3248 —— 3200
   3291 —— 3300
   3462 —— 3500
   3555 —— 3600
9. **a)** 7480 m   **b)** 3070 m
10. **a)** 320
    b) 420

Test 5
1. **a)** 0.7   **b)** 0.3   **c)** 0.8
2. 0.1   0.4   0.7   0.8
3. **a)** $\frac{1}{10}$ **b)** $\frac{6}{10}$ **c)** $\frac{9}{10}$
4. $8.3 - 8\frac{3}{10}$
   $9.7 - 9\frac{7}{10}$
   $8.1 - 8\frac{1}{10}$
   $9.4 - 9\frac{4}{10}$
   $8.9 - 8\frac{9}{10}$
5. 2.1   2.3   2.6   2.9
6. $0.35 - \frac{35}{100}$
   $0.04 - \frac{4}{100}$
   $0.55 - \frac{55}{100}$
   $0.44 - \frac{44}{100}$
   $0.53 - \frac{53}{100}$
7. **a)** 0.37   **b)** 0.85   **c)** 0.09
8. £6.08   £6.45   £6.54
   £6.58   £6.80
9. 0.02   0.06   0.14   0.18
10. 57.39

Test 6
1. **a)** $\frac{4}{5}$ **b)** $\frac{3}{10}$ **c)** $\frac{5}{6}$
2. Three parts of each shape should be shaded.
3.
4. Check the circle has approximately $\frac{2}{3}$ shaded.
5. $\frac{4}{5}$
6. **a)** $\frac{5}{8}$ **b)** $\frac{2}{5}$ **c)** $\frac{7}{10}$
7. **a)** $\frac{2}{5}$ **b)** $\frac{1}{6}$
8. **a)** Five parts should be shaded.
   b) Two parts should be shaded.
9. **a)** $\frac{3}{7} < \frac{5}{7}$ **b)** $\frac{1}{3} > \frac{1}{5}$
10.

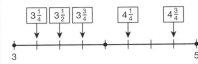

Test 7
1. **a)** $\frac{1}{3} = \frac{2}{6}$ **b)** $\frac{1}{4} = \frac{3}{12}$
2. **a)** $\frac{1}{2} = \frac{5}{10}$ **b)** $\frac{1}{3} = \frac{4}{12}$
3. **a)** $\frac{1}{5} = \frac{3}{15}$ **b)** $\frac{1}{4} = \frac{4}{16}$
4. $\frac{6}{15}$
5. $\frac{4}{10}$
6. **a)** Nine parts should be shaded $\left(\frac{9}{12}\right)$.
   b) Six parts should be shaded $\left(\frac{6}{8}\right)$.
7. $\frac{1}{3} = \frac{2}{6} = \frac{3}{9} = \frac{4}{12} = \frac{5}{15}$
8. $\frac{3}{4} = \frac{6}{8}$
9. $\frac{2}{3} = \frac{4}{6}$
10. $\frac{4}{5} = \frac{8}{10}$

Test 8
1. 6 red, 4 blue
2. 12 red, 8 blue
3. 9 red, 6 blue
4. Check that there are 8 green squares and 4 yellow squares.
5. Check that there are 8 green squares and 2 yellow squares.
6. Check pattern shows 6 black tiles and 12 white tiles.
7. Check pattern shows 12 black tiles and 18 white tiles.
8. Check pattern shows 18 black tiles and 6 white tiles.
9. 10
10. 12

Test 9
1. **a)** 60   **b)** 90
2. **a)** 70   **b)** 80
3. **a)** 500   **b)** 200
   c) 700   **d)** 400
4. **a)** 9   **b)** 15
   c) 9   **d)** 15
5.

+	90	60	80
70	160	**130**	150
40	130	**100**	120
50	**140**	110	**130**

6. 160
7. **a)** 120   **b)** 60   **c)** 140
8. 800 → 300 → 100 → 15
9.

IN	150	**110**	190	**130**	120
OUT	**80**	40	**120**	60	**50**

10. 70

Test 10

1. **a)** 3   **b)** 8   **c)** 7
2. $7 \times 6 = \mathbf{42}$
   $6 \times 7 = \mathbf{42}$
   $\mathbf{42} \div 6 = \mathbf{7}$
   $\mathbf{42} \div 7 = \mathbf{6}$
3. **a)** 36   **b)** 40   **c)** 49
4. **a)** 7   **b)** 7   **c)** 9
5.

×	4	**5**	8
9	**36**	45	**72**
7	**28**	**35**	**56**
3	12	**15**	**24**

6. **a)** 48 → any from 1×48,
   2×24, 3×16, 4×12, 6×8
   b) 60 → any from 1×60,
   2×30, 3×20, 4×15,
   5×12, 6×10
7. 36
8. 7
9. 45
10. Remainder 1 → $57 \div 8$ and
    $41 \div 2$
    Remainder 2 → $50 \div 3$ and
    $38 \div 6$
    Remainder 3 → $48 \div 5$ and
    $83 \div 10$
    Remainder 4 → $46 \div 6$ and
    $89 \div 5$
    Remainder 5 → $65 \div 6$ and
    $68 \div 9$

Test 11

1. **a)** 79   **b)** 117   **c)** 155
2. 46 and 58
3. 38 and 63
4. **a)** $87 + \mathbf{28} = 115$
   b) $\mathbf{49} + 74 = 123$
5. $135 + 65$
   $95 + 105$
   $128 + 72$
   $138 + 62$
6. 150 km
7. **a)** 447   **b)** 566   **c)** 731
8. **a)**

62	53	**115**
29	47	**76**
91	**100**	**191**

   b)

49	58	**107**
71	93	**164**
120	**151**	**271**

9. **a)** $3\mathbf{6}5 + 289 = \mathbf{6}54$
   b) $\mathbf{4}49 + 376 = 82\mathbf{5}$
10. £43.05

Test 12

1. **a)** 59   **b)** 36
2.

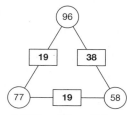

3. **a)** $2\mathbf{4}3 - 82 = 1\mathbf{6}1$
   b) $3\mathbf{9}2 - 57 = \mathbf{3}35$
4. 93
5. $67 - 122$
   $92 - 147$
   $142 - 87$
6. **a)** $82 - \mathbf{58} = 24$
   b) $76 - 49 = 27$
   c) $77 - 38 = 39$
   d) $95 - \mathbf{69} = 26$
7. **a)** 29   **b)** 72
8. 158
9. $340 - 29 →\mathbf{311} - 29 →$
   $\mathbf{282} - 29 → \mathbf{253} - 29 → \mathbf{224}$
10. **a)** 175   **b)** 219   **c)** 254

Test 13

1.

IN	14	**30**	22	**17**	40
OUT	**1400**	3000	**2200**	1700	**4000**

2. 11
3. **a)** 145   **b)** 204
4. 168 hours
5. **a)** 560   **b)** 940
6. **a)** 342   **b)** 756
7. £228
8. **a)** 360   **b)** 476   **c)** 332
9. 1320
10. 270

Test 14

1. **a)** 9   **b)** 23
   c) 7   **d)** 13
2. **a)** 54   **b)** 73   **c)** 67
3.

IN	370	900	740	810	620
OUT	**37**	**90**	**74**	**81**	**62**

4. **a)** 12   **b)** 18
   c) 14
5. **a)** 35   **b)** 56
   c) 9   **d)** 9
6. 8 pencils
   2 pencils left over
7. **a)** 18 r 1   **b)** 11 r 4
8. 13
9. **a)** $35 \div 7 = \mathbf{5}$
   b) $56 \div 4 = \mathbf{14}$
   c) $\mathbf{72} \div 3 = 24$
   d) $\mathbf{60} \div 5 = 12$
10. 4

Test 15

3	6	1	4	5
2	3	2	2	5
1	5	8	2	0
8	2	1	4	1
4	8	8	5	6

Test 16

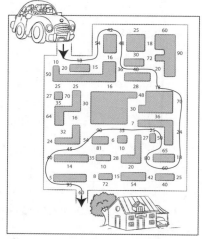

Alternative answers are possible.

Test 17

1. 5
2. **a)** $\frac{1}{5}$ of…
   $15 → 3$
   $30 → 6$
   $20 → 4$
   $25 → 5$
   b) $\frac{1}{3}$ of…
   $12 → 4$
   $21 → 7$
   $18 → 6$
   $30 → 10$
3. 75 g
4. Check grid is coloured
   correctly (18 squares blue,
   9 squares yellow, 6 squares red)
5. $\frac{1}{12}$
6. 12
7. 6 litres
8. **a)** $\frac{2}{3}$ of $24 = 16$
   b) $\frac{3}{4}$ of $24 = 18$
   c) $\frac{5}{6}$ of $24 = 20$
   d) $\frac{3}{8}$ of $24 = 9$
9. $\frac{3}{5}$ of 15 litres
10. **a)** 28   **b)** 63   **c)** 77

Test 18

1.

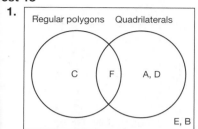

2.

3. 8

4. isosceles triangle

5. Sometimes true – a square is a special rectangle with four equal sides.

6.

All *quadrilaterals* have four sides.

7.

All *heptagons* have seven sides.

8.

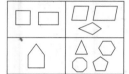

9. equilateral triangle

10. Sometimes true – regular pentagons have five equal sides.

Test 19

1.

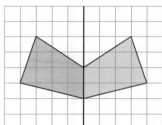

2. Yes

3. Answers may vary but could include:

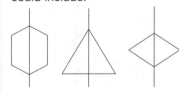

4.

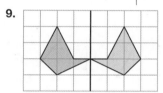

5. four lines of symmetry

6. P

7. B

8.

9.

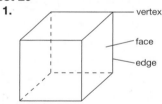

10. rectangle

Test 20

1.

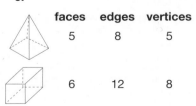

2. cylinder

3. cuboids

4. (square-based) pyramid

5.

tetrahedron →

cube →

cuboid →

square-based pyramid →

6.

	faces	edges	vertices
	5	8	5
	6	12	8

7. cone   cylinder

8. 4

9. sphere

10. 9

Test 21

1–5.

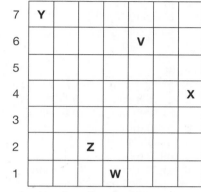

	A	B	C	D	E	F	G
7	Y						
6					V		
5							
4							X
3							
2			Z				
1				W			

6. triangle → F5

7. circle → B3

8. rectangle → C7

9. pentagon → A1

10. square → G2

Test 22

1.

2. Check angle is greater than 90°.

3.

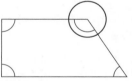

4. West

5. 360°

6.

7.

8. false

9. 44° or 45°

10.

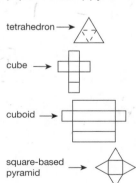

Test 23

1. 20 mm

2. 5 cm 50 mm
6 cm 60 mm
9 cm 90 mm

3. 175 mm   210 mm
242 mm   280 mm

4. 2500 metres

5. 7.5 km or 7500 m
6. 40 mm   55 mm
7. 15 mm
8. a) 580 m
   b) 270 m
9. The length of a pen is about 15 cm.
10. a) 1500 m
    b) 6.5 m
    c) 95 mm
    d) 2.8 km

Test 24
1. a) 700 ml b) 1600 ml c) 1200 ml
2. a) 1500 ml   b) 2.25 litres
   c) 5700 ml   d) 6.8 litres
3. 2300 ml
4. 4 jugfuls
5. 4900 ml
6. a) 3900 ml   b) 9.8 litres
   c) 10 000 ml   d) 7.25 litres
7. 400 ml
8. 0.3 litres
9. 500 ml
10. a) 7 litres 330 ml
    b) 6 litres 50 ml
    c) 8 litres 200 ml
    d) 3 litres 145 ml

Test 25
1. 1100 g
2. a) 4500 g   b) 8600 g
   c) 3250 g
3. 14
4. 1300 g
5. 1400 g
6. a) 400 g b) 290 g   c) 1600 g
7. 400 g
8. 17
9. a) 1 kg 930 g   b) 6 kg 50 g
   c) 7 kg 320 g   d) 5 kg 945 g
10. 3.8 kg

Test 26
1. 14 squares
2. Check that the rectangle has a perimeter of 14 squares.
   (1 × 6, 2 × 5 or 3 × 4)
3. 5 cm
4. 20 squares
5. 32 cm
6. Check that each shape has an area of 9 squares.

7. 24 squares
8. 4 cm
9. Check that the rectangle has a perimeter of 18 squares.
   (3 × 6, 4 × 5, 2 × 7 or 1 × 8)
10. 236 mm

Test 27
1. a) 8:55   b) 11:05
   c) 1:20   d) 3:25
2. 8.20 p.m.
3. a) 5 minutes
   b) 150 seconds
   c) 270 minutes
   d) 10 days
4. a) 2:28   b) 7:07
   c) 12:33   d) 5:48
5. 6.55 a.m.
6. 2.40 p.m.
7. 2 hours 55 minutes
8. Monday 30th June

9.

Ancaster	9.40 a.m.	**11.15 a.m.**	**12.45 p.m.**
Bidsbury	**10.15 a.m.**	11.50 a.m.	**1.20 p.m.**
Collerton	10.50 a.m.	**12.25 p.m.**	1.55 p.m

10. 12:07

Test 28
1. Friday
2. 13
3. Tuesday
4. 7
5. 114
6. 7
7. March
8. 5
9. January, July, October
10. false (29 books in first 6 months; 36 books in second 6 months)

Test 29
1. triangle
2. square
3. circle
4. rectangle
5. pentagon
6. hexagon

Test 30
Check that the ship is symmetrical (see diagram below) and shaded.

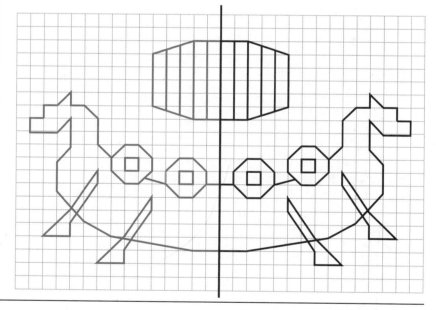

Published by Letts Educational
An imprint of HarperCollins*Publishers*
77–85 Fulham Palace Road
London W6 8JB
Telephone: 0844 576 8126
Fax: 0844 576 8131
Email: education@harpercollins.co.uk
Website: www.lettsrevision.com

ISBN 9781844197224

First published in 2013

Text © Paul Broadbent

Design and illustration © 2013 Letts Educational, an imprint of HarperCollins*Publishers*

Every effort has been made to trace copyright holders and obtain their permission for the use of copyright material. The author and publisher will gladly receive information enabling them to rectify any error or omission in subsequent editions. All facts are correct at time of going to press.

Division

6. 50 pencils are shared equally into six pots.

How many pencils are in each pot? _____

How many pencils are left over? _____

7. Answer these.

a) $73 \div 4 =$ _____ r _____

b) $92 \div 8 =$ _____ r _____

8. A box holds four light bulbs. How many boxes are needed for 49 light bulbs?

_____

9. Write the missing digits 1 to 6 to complete these divisions correctly. Use each digit only once.

| 1 | 2 | 3 | 4 | 5 | 6 |

a) [   ] $5 \div 7 =$ [   ]

b) $56 \div$ [   ] $=$ [   ] 4

c) 7 [   ] $\div 3 = 24$

d) [   ] $0 \div 5 = 12$

10. What is the remainder when 100 is divided by 6?

_____

/10

Multiplication puzzle

Write the answers to this number puzzle. Only one digit should be written in each square.

1		2	3	
	4		5	6
7		8	9	
	10			11
12		13	14	

Clues

Across

1. 6×6

3. 9×5

4. 8×4

5. 2×1

7. 3×5

9. 5×4

10. 3×7

12. 6×8

13. 4×2

14. 7×8

Down

1. 4×8

2. 3×4

3. 6×7

4. 7×5

6. 5×10

7. 3×6

8. 9×9

9. 6×4

10. 4×7

11. 4×4

Multiples maze

Find the way home. You can only travel on roads which are multiples of 5 or 6. Colour the route you take.

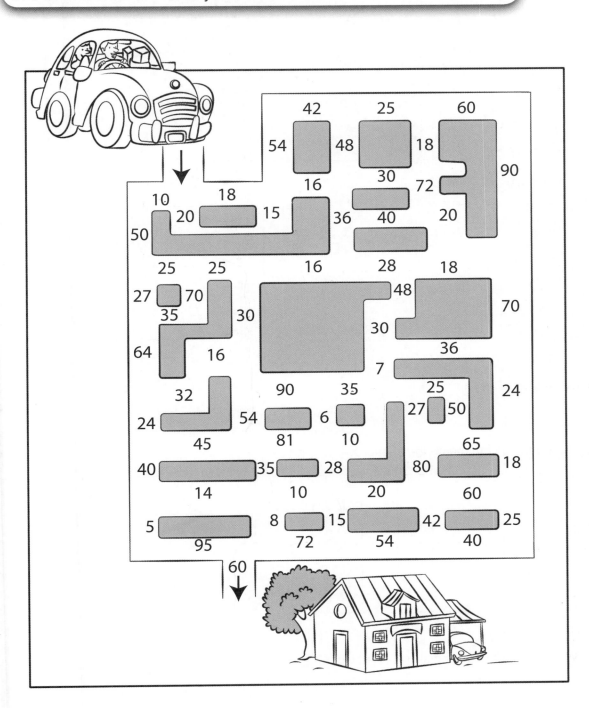

Fractions of quantities

1. Colour $\frac{1}{4}$ of these stars and write the answer.

$\frac{1}{4}$ of 20 = ⬜

2. Answer each of these.

a)
$\frac{1}{5}$ of...

15 → _____

30 → _____

20 → _____

25 → _____

b)
$\frac{1}{3}$ of...

12 → _____

21 → _____

18 → _____

30 → _____

3. What is $\frac{3}{4}$ of 100 g?

_____ g

4. Colour the grid to match the fractions.

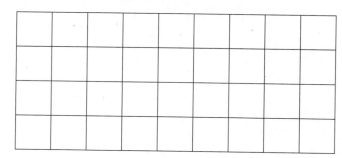

$\frac{1}{2}$ → blue

$\frac{1}{6}$ → red

$\frac{1}{4}$ → yellow

5. What fraction of the grid above is left white?

_____

6. Colour $\frac{2}{3}$ of the circles and write the answer.

$\frac{2}{3}$ of 18 =

7. A water tank holds 20 litres when it is full. How much water is in the tank when it is $\frac{3}{10}$ full?

_____ litres

8. Answer these.

a) $\frac{2}{3}$ of 24 =

b) $\frac{3}{4}$ of 24 =

c) $\frac{5}{6}$ of 24 =

d) $\frac{3}{8}$ of 24 =

9. Circle the largest amount.

$\frac{2}{3}$ of 12 litres

$\frac{3}{5}$ of 15 litres

10. What is $\frac{7}{10}$ of each of these numbers?

a) 40 →

b) 90 →

c) 110 →

/10

1. Sort the shapes. Write the letters in the correct parts of this Venn diagram.

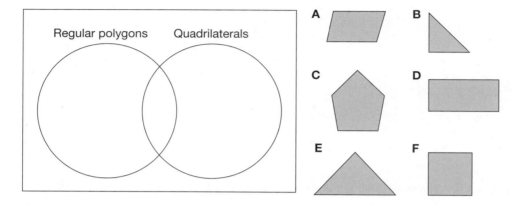

Regular polygons   Quadrilaterals

A   B   C   D   E   F

2. Tick the pentagons in this set of shapes.

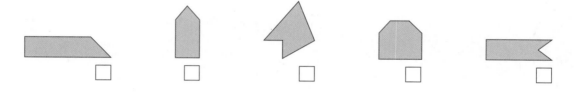

☐   ☐   ☐   ☐   ☐

3. How many sides does an octagon have?

_____

4. Name this shape.

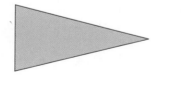

_____

5. A rectangle has four equal-length sides. Is this always, sometimes or never true?

_____

6. Cross out the odd shape. Complete the sentence.

All _____ have four sides.

7. Cross out the odd shape. Complete the sentence.

All _____ have seven sides.

8. Draw lines to join each shape to the correct place on this Carroll diagram.

Right angles   No right angles

Quadrilateral

Not a quadrilateral

9. Which shape has three equal sides and three equal angles?

_____

10. A pentagon has five equal-length sides. Is this always, sometimes or never true?

_____

/10

Symmetry

1. Draw the reflection of this shape.

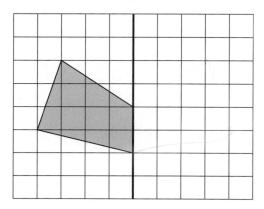

2. Is an isosceles triangle symmetrical? Circle your answer.   Yes / No

3. Draw a line of reflection on each shape.

4. Draw the reflection of this shape.

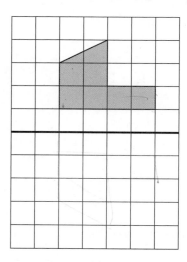

5. How many lines of symmetry does a square have?

_____

6. Cross out the letter that is **not** symmetrical.

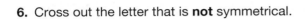

C H T A P M

7. Which square tile, A, B or C, is a reflection of the first tile?

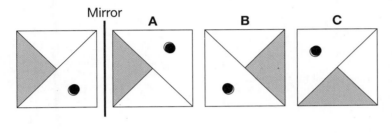

Mirror A B C

_____

8. Draw lines of symmetry on these shapes.

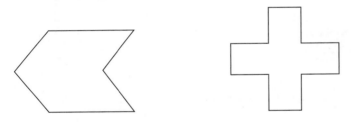

9. Draw the reflection of this shape.

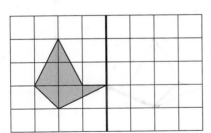

10. Name this shape:

A quadrilateral with two lines of symmetry and four right angles.

_____

/10

3-D shapes

1. Label the parts of this cube.

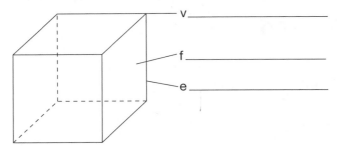

v_____

f_____

e_____

2. Cross out the odd one out from this set of shapes.

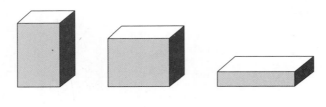

What is the name of the shape you crossed out?

_____

3. What type of 3-D shapes have been left showing in question 2?

_____

4. Name this shape.

_____

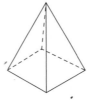

5. These nets will fold to make 3-D shapes. Draw lines to match each net to the name of its shape.

tetrahedron   cube   cuboid   square-based pyramid

3-D shapes

6. Write how many faces, edges and vertices each shape has.

	faces	edges	vertices

_____ _____ _____

_____ _____ _____

7. The 3-D shapes below pass through these holes.

Name each 3-D shape if these are the side views of them.

shape: _____

shape: _____

8. How many triangle faces does a triangular pyramid, or tetrahedron, have?

_____

9. Name this 3-D shape.

_____

10. How many edges does a triangular prism have?

/10

_____

Coordinates

Write the letters in the correct squares on the grid.

1. Z → C2

2. Y → A7

3. X → G4

4. W → D1

5. V → E6

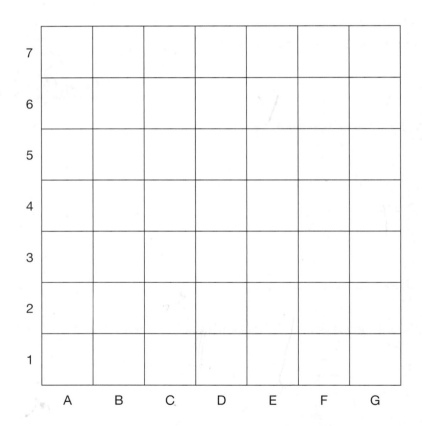

Coordinates

Write the position on the grid of each shape.

6. triangle → _____

7. circle → _____

8. rectangle → _____

9. pentagon → _____

10. square → _____

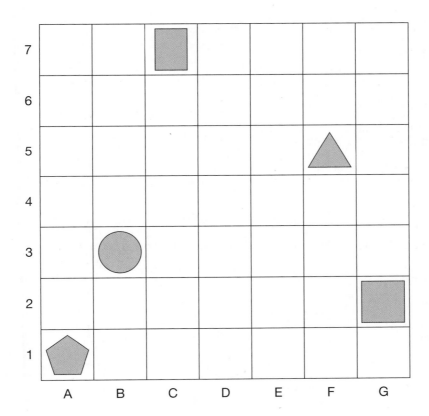

/10

Angles

1. Circle the two angles that are the same.

2. Draw an angle greater than 90° on this grid.

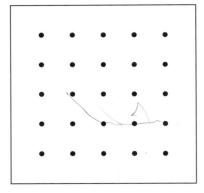

3. Circle the largest angle in this shape.

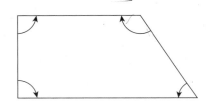

4. A man is facing East. He turns 180° clockwise. In which direction is he now facing?

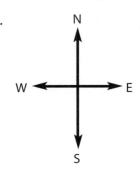

_____

5. How many degrees are there in a complete circle?

_____ °

6. Circle the smallest angle in this set.

7. This arrow is rotated 90° anti-clockwise. Tick the arrow that is now pointing in the correct direction.

8. True or false? An 80° angle is greater than a right angle.

_____

9. Use a protractor or angle measurer to measure this angle.

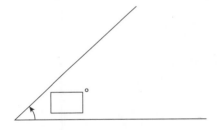

10. Tick the angle that shows 60°.

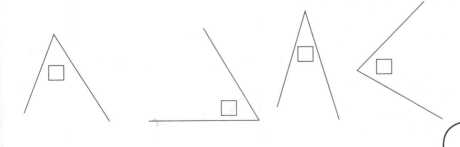

/10

Measuring length

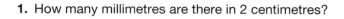

1. How many millimetres are there in 2 centimetres?

   _____ mm

2. Write the length of each line in centimetres and millimetres.

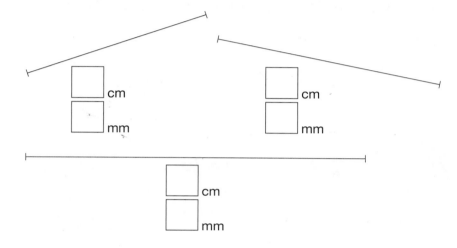

3. Write the lengths, in millimetres, shown by each arrow on this ruler.

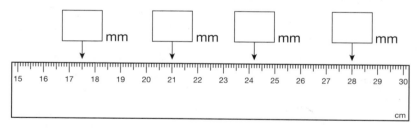

4. How many metres are there in 2.5 kilometres?

   _____ metres

5. What is 500 m less than 8 km?

   _____ km or _____ m

Measuring length

6. Measure these pencils and write their lengths in millimetres.

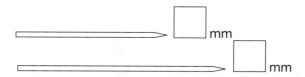 mm

mm

7. What is the difference in length between these two lines?

mm

mm

Difference = _____ mm

8. What must be added to each measurement to make 1 kilometre?

a) 420 m + _____ m

b) 730 m + _____ m

9. Tick the correct value to complete the sentence.

The length of a pen is about…

1.5 cm ☐

15 cm ☐

150 cm ☐

1500 cm ☐

10. Write these lengths.

a) 1.5 km = _____ m

b) 650 cm = _____ m

c) 9.5 cm = _____ mm

d) 2800 m = _____ km

/10

Measuring capacity

1. Write how much liquid is in each container.

   a)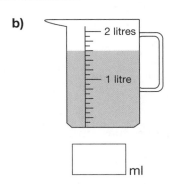

   ☐ ml

   b)

   ☐ ml

   c)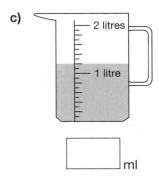

   ☐ ml

2. Complete these.

   a) $1\frac{1}{2}$ litres = _____ ml

   b) 2250 ml = _____ litres

   c) 5.7 litres = _____ ml

   d) 6800 ml = _____ litres

3. What is the total amount in these two jugs?

   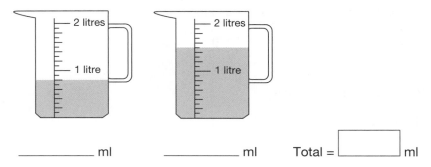

   _____ ml   _____ ml   Total = ☐ ml

4. How many 750 ml jugfuls will fill a 3-litre bucket?

   _____

5. Round this amount to the nearest 100 ml.

   ☐ ml

Measuring capacity

6. Complete these.

    a) 3.9 litres = _____ ml

    b) 9800 ml = _____ litres

    c) 10 litres = _____ ml

    d) 7250 ml = _____ litres

7. What is the difference in the amounts in these two jugs?

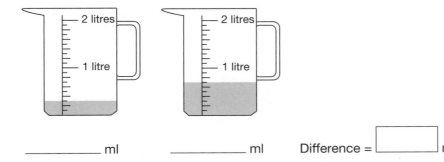

_____ ml   _____ ml   Difference = ☐ ml

8. Tick the correct value to complete the sentence.

    A can of drink holds about…

    5 litres   ☐

    0.3 litres   ☐

    30 litres   ☐

    500 litres   ☐

9. A jug holds 2 litres of water. If three-quarters of the water is poured out, how much is left in the jug?

    _____ ml

10. Write these as litres and millilitres.

    a) 7330 ml = _____ litres _____ ml

    b) 6050 ml = _____ litres _____ ml

    c) 8200 ml = _____ litres _____ ml

    d) 3145 ml = _____ litres _____ ml

/10

Measuring weight

1. Write the weight of this parcel in grams.

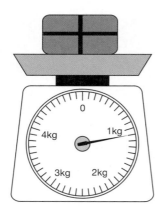

_____ g

2. Complete these.

   a) 4.5 kg = _____ g   **b)** 8.6 kg = _____ g   **c)** 3.25 kg = _____ g

3. How many 250 g weights will balance 3.5 kg?

_____

4. What is the difference in weight between these two parcels?

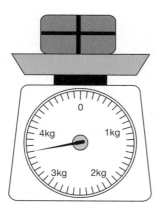 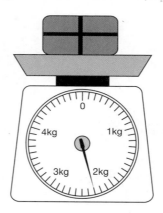

_____   _____   Difference = ☐ g

5. A cake weighs 1385 g. What is this rounded to the nearest 100 g?

_____ g

Measuring weight

6. Write these in grams.

a)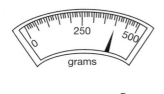

_____ g

b)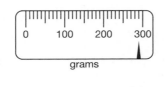

_____ g

c)

_____ g

7. What weight is shown on this scale, to the nearest 100 g?

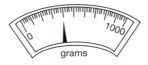

_____ g

8. How many 0.5 kg weights will balance 8.5 kg?

_____

9. Complete these.

a) 1930 g = _____ kg _____ g   **b)** 6050 g = _____ kg _____ g

c) 7320 g = _____ kg _____ g   **d)** 5945 g = _____ kg _____ g

10. What is the total weight of these parcels?

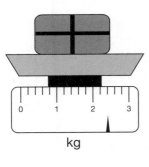

_____   _____   Total = ☐ kg

/10

Area and perimeter

1. What is the area of this shape?

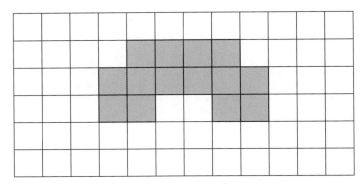

Area = _____ squares

2. Use the grid lines to draw a rectangle with a perimeter of 14 squares.

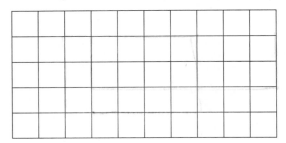

3. A square has a perimeter of 20 cm. What is the length of each side? _____ cm

4. What is the area of this shape?

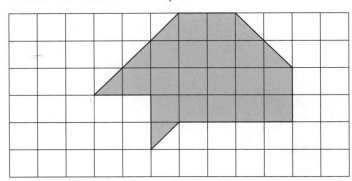

Area = _____ squares

5. A rectangle has sides of 6.5 cm and 9.5 cm. What is the perimeter of the rectangle?

9.5 cm

6.5 cm

_____ cm

Area and perimeter

6. Draw two different shapes on this grid, each with an area of 9 squares.

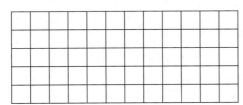

7. What is the approximate area of this shape? Tick your answer.

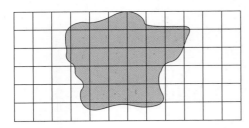

17 squares ☐

45 squares ☐

24 squares ☐

32 squares ☐

8. A square has an area of 16 square centimetres.

What is the length of each side?

Area = 16 square centimetres

Length of side = _____ cm

9. Draw a rectangle on this grid with a perimeter of 18 squares.

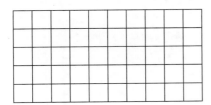

10. What is the perimeter of this rectangle?

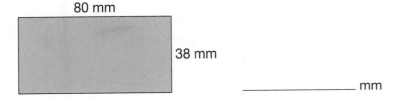

80 mm

38 mm

_____ mm

/10

Time

1. Write these times.

a)

:

b)

:

c)

:

d)

:

2. A film starts at 6.40 p.m. and lasts for 1 hour 40 minutes.

What time does the film end? Write your answer using a.m. or p.m.

_____

3. Complete these.

a) 300 seconds = _____ minutes

b) $2\frac{1}{2}$ minutes = _____ seconds

c) $4\frac{1}{2}$ hours = _____ minutes

d) 240 hours = _____ days

4. Write these times.

a)

:

b)

:

c)

:

d)

:

5. The time is now 7.25 a.m. I woke up half an hour ago.

What time was it when I woke up? Write your answer using a.m. or p.m.

_____

6. If the time is 9.40 a.m., what time will it be in five hours? Write your answer using a.m. or p.m.

_____

7. How many hours and minutes are there between these two times?

☐ hours ☐ minutes

8. If today is Tuesday 1st July, what date was it yesterday?

_____

9. A coach takes 35 minutes between each stop. Complete the timetable.

Ancaster	9.40 a.m.		
Bidsbury		11.50 a.m.	
Collerton	10.50 a.m.		1.55 p.m.

10. My watch shows 11:52, but it is 15 minutes slow. What is the actual time?

_____

/10

Tables, charts and graphs

This table shows a record of the number of visitors to a school website each day.

Monday	ⅢⅠ ⅢⅠ ⅢⅠ ⅢⅠ ǁ	
Tuesday	ⅢⅠ ⅢⅠ ⅢⅠ	
Wednesday	ⅢⅠ ⅢⅠ ⅢⅠ ⅢⅠ ⅢⅠ ǁǁǁǁ	
Thursday	ⅢⅠ ⅢⅠ ǁǁǁ	
Friday	ⅢⅠ ⅢⅠ ⅢⅠ ⅢⅠ ⅢⅠ ⅢⅠ ⅢⅠ	

ⅢⅠ stands for 5 visitors

1. Which day had the most visitors?

_____

2. How many visits to the website were there on Thursday?

_____

3. On which day did 15 people visit the website?

_____

4. How many more visitors were there on Wednesday than on Monday?

_____

5. How many visitors to the website were there in total?

_____

Tables, charts and graphs

This graph shows the number of books read by Sam each month for a year.

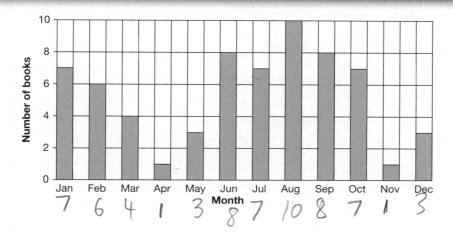

7 6 4 1 3 8 7 10 8 7 1 3

6. How many books did Sam read in July?

_____

7. In which month did he read four books?

_____

8. How many more books did Sam read in September than in May?

_____

9. In which three months did he read the same number of books?

_____

10. Sam read more books in the first six months than in the second six months of the year.
True or false?

_____

/10

Shape puzzle

Trace a path through the grid to find the names of six shapes. Only visit each letter once. Write the shapes in the order you find them.

Start	T	R	N	G	U	A	R	E
N	O	I	A	L	Q	R	I	C
H	G	A	T	E	S	C	L	E
E	X	A	N	E	L	A	T	R
N	O	G	E	P	G	N	C	E

1. _____

2. _____

3. _____

4. _____

5. _____

6. _____

Symmetrical fun

Draw and colour this ship so that it is symmetrical.
Use a ruler to draw the lines.

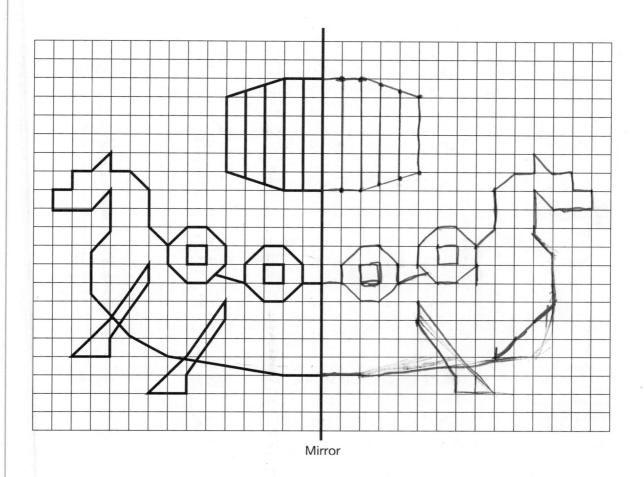

Mirror

Progress report

Colour each box in the correct colour to show how many questions you got right.

0–2 = yellow, 3–5 = green, 6–7 = blue, 8–10 = red

This will help you to monitor your progress.

Test 1 /10 Date _____	**Test 2** /10 Date _____	**Test 3** /10 Date _____	**Test 4** /10 Date _____	**Test 5** /10 Date _____
Test 6 /10 Date _____	**Test 7** /10 Date _____	**Test 8** /10 Date _____	**Test 9** /10 Date _____	**Test 10** /10 Date _____
Test 11 /10 Date _____	**Test 12** /10 Date _____	**Test 13** /10 Date _____	**Test 14** /10 Date _____	**Test 15** If you did the puzzle in less than 10 minutes, colour this red. If you took longer, colour this blue. Date _____
Test 16 Did you finish the maze? If you did it in less than 10 minutes, colour this red. If you took longer, colour this blue. Date _____	**Test 17** /10 Date _____	**Test 18** /10 Date _____	**Test 19** /10 Date _____	**Test 20** /10 Date _____
Test 21 /10 Date _____	**Test 22** /10 Date _____	**Test 23** /10 Date _____	**Test 24** /10 Date _____	**Test 25** /10 Date _____
Test 26 /10 Date _____	**Test 27** /10 Date _____	**Test 28** /10 Date _____	**Test 29** If you complete the puzzle, then colour this red. Date _____	**Test 30** If you complete the ship, then colour this red. Date _____